Sea Side Trippers

A Minidrama

Richard Tydeman

A Samuel French Acting Edition

FOUNDED 1830

SAMUELFRENCH-LONDON.CO.UK
SAMUELFRENCH.COM

Copyright © 1957 by Richard Tydeman
All Rights Reserved

SEA SIDE TRIPPERS is fully protected under the copyright laws of the British Commonwealth, including Canada, the United States of America, and all other countries of the Copyright Union. All rights, including professional and amateur stage productions, recitation, lecturing, public reading, motion picture, radio broadcasting, television and the rights of translation into foreign languages are strictly reserved.

ISBN 978-0-573-13305-3

www.samuelfrench-london.co.uk

www.samuelfrench.com

FOR AMATEUR PRODUCTION ENQUIRIES

UNITED KINGDOM AND WORLD EXCLUDING NORTH AMERICA

plays@SamuelFrench-London.co.uk

020 7255 4302/01

Each title is subject to availability from Samuel French,

depending upon country of performance.

CAUTION: Professional and amateur producers are hereby warned that *SEA SIDE TRIPPERS* is subject to a licensing fee. Publication of this play does not imply availability for performance. Both amateurs and professionals considering a production are strongly advised to apply to the appropriate agent before starting rehearsals, advertising, or booking a theatre. A licensing fee must be paid whether the title is presented for charity or gain and whether or not admission is charged.

The professional rights in this play are controlled by Samuel French Ltd, 52 Fitzroy Street, London, W1T 5JR.

No one shall make any changes in this title for the purpose of production. No part of this book may be reproduced, stored in a retrieval system, or transmitted in any form, by any means, now known or yet to be invented, including mechanical, electronic, photocopying, recording, videotaping, or otherwise, without the prior written permission of the publisher. No one shall upload this title, or part of this title, to any social media websites.

The right of Richard Tydeman to be identified as author of this work has been asserted by him in accordance with Section 77 of the Copyright, Designs and Patents Act 1988

Characters

The Announcer
The Oldest Resident
The Second Oldest Resident
The Trippers, including The Young One, The
    Informative One, The Cheery One, The
    Gloomy One, The Anxious One, The
    Knitter, The Mother, The President, The
    Secretary, The Adventurous One, The
    Hungry One and The Reader

Scene: A secluded bay on the sea-coast, just before lunch

In response to the request of many teams for a successor to the same author's *Spring Song Singers*, this minidrama has been written in similar style, for the same selection of characters, and is just as easy to learn and produce, but it is in no sense a sequel and is quite complete in itself. Only two people have more than twelve lines - and one of those has a book!

SEA SIDE TRIPPERS

The scene represents a secluded bay on the sea-coast. The backcloth or back wall of the stage represents cliffs; the stage is the beach; the footlights mark the water's edge, and the audience is in the sea. Up R. are some high rocks and in front of them some low rocks. L. is a single low rock. These rocks consist of tables, chairs and boxes, covered with black or coloured cloths.

Down R. in a deck chair sits the OLDEST RESIDENT. *Down L., in another deck chair, sits the* SECOND OLDEST RESIDENT. *They are turned away from the audience, wrapped in rugs, etc., with sunshades or canopies or newspapers to hide their heads. They are both fast asleep.*

Before the curtain rises, THE ANNOUNCER *appears before the curtain—or the* ANNOUNCER'S *voice can be heard over the theatre's loudspeakers.*

ANNOUNCER (*in the exaggerated style of the introduction to an American travel film*). Come with me now to a beautiful and secluded little bay on the sea coast of sunny England. (*Or, of course, sunny Scotland, Wales, Jersey, Tasmania, or where you like.*)

(The Curtain rises.)

Far from the noisy roar of the mighty city, the two oldest residents from the exclusive Guest House enjoy the quiet beauty of a summer's day. Above them the mighty cliffs afford shelter from the wayward wind. Around them stand old and weather-beaten rocks; beneath them lies the sand and shingle beach; and you, my friends, are all, of course, under the sea.

Let us pause awhile and contemplate the beauties of this lovely, lonely, fascinating spot. (*Exit.*)

OLDEST RESIDENT (*waking up and leaning out of chair*). I say. (*Pause.*) Er—I say. Oh well, if you are asleep it doesn't matter. (*Settles back and goes to sleep.*)

SECOND OLDEST RESIDENT (*stirring sleepily after a pause*). Eh? What was that? (*Looking round.*) I thought somebody said something. (*Goes to sleep again.*)

OLDEST RESIDENT (*stirring after a pause*). Ah, you've woken up, have you? (*Leans across.*) I was only going to say—(*No movement from the other.*) Oh well, it doesn't matter. (*Goes to sleep again.*)

(Enter up L., the first of the TRIPPERS, THE YOUNG ONE, *who looks all round, then beckons off stage and calls.*)

YOUNG. Oo—oo! Everybody! Come down here; there's a lovely bit of sand. Oh come on! There's only a couple of—(*Breaks off and looks intently at the two in the deck chairs.*) there's only a couple

SEA SIDE TRIPPERS

of old geysers fast asleep. Mind how you come down the path, it's a bit slippery. Throw some of the things down; I'll catch them. Ready now.

(Various bundles are thrown on from up L., apparently from further up the cliff. Coats, towels, bathing costumes, brown paper parcels, beach balls, cushions and rugs—the more the merrier. The Young One *comments on these ad lib., as they arrive.)*

Is that the lot?

(Turns and bends over the heap. A final bundle—perhaps a rolled up mattress or large cushion, knocks Young One *on to the heap.)*

Hey!

(Enter several of the Trippers, *up* L. *In spite of the things thrown down, they are all heavily laden with bags, baskets, coats, umbrellas, stools, etc. First to enter are* The Informative One, The Cheery One *and* The Gloomy One, *followed by* The Anxious One *and* The Knitter.*)*

Informative *(moving down* R.*).* Ah, this is the little cove that the Guide Book mentions. Now where did I see it? *(Turns pages of guide book.)*

Cheery *(moving down* L.*).* Well, here we are at the seaside at last. *(Looking round.)* Ooh, isn't it lovely!

Gloomy (L.C.). We should have done better to go to Clacton. *(Or "Blackpool" or some other well-known resort.)*

Informative. We went there last year, and you complained because of the crowds.

Knitter *(mounting high rock and sitting, counting stitches on an enormous piece of knitting).* 34, 35, 36, 37 . . .

Anxious *(up* C.*)* Oh dear, do you think it's going to rain?

Informative *(reading from guide book).* This particular part of the coast is noted for its humid atmosphere and has a high average rainfall.

Cheery. Rain? Of course it won't rain. It never rains on the Club Outing. *(For "Club" insert the name of any organisation widely represented in the audience.)*

Gloomy. Huh! Two years ago at Skegness *(Or where you like.)* we got soaked to the skin, *(To* Informative.*)* didn't we?

Informative *(doubtfully).* Yes, only technically that wasn't the Club Outing, it was the Institute *(Or some other organisation.),* and it was Cleethorpes not Skegness, and it was three years ago, not two.

Knitter. 53, 54, 55, 56 . . .

Cheery *(gazing out over audience).* Just look at the sea, sparkling away in the sunshine, and as smooth as a millpond. Who's coming to have a paddle?

Anxious. Oh dear, is it safe, do you think?

Gloomy. Wasn't it about here that those two men got sucked under by the current last summer?

SEA SIDE TRIPPERS

ANXIOUS (*drawing back*). Oh, was it?
GLOOMY (*with relish*). They only recovered one of the bodies. (ANXIOUS *squeals.*) Isn't that right?
INFORMATIVE. Yes, only of course it was a bit further up the coast, and there were four of them, and it was in the great storm in January.
GLOOMY (*to* ANXIOUS). There you are, you see.
KNITTER. 78, 79, 80, 81 . . .
INFORMATIVE (*reading*). From the beach it is possible to obtain views of the distant islands. On a clear day when visibility is good—
YOUNG (*coming down* C.). Oh, look at that ship.
ALL. Where? Where?
YOUNG (*pointing out over audience*). There. You can only just see it. It's going over the horizon.
ANXIOUS. Is it sinking?
YOUNG. Of course not. (*Sits on floor down* R.)
GLOOMY. You can't tell. I wouldn't go over that horizon for a fortune.
CHEERY. Why not?
GLOOMY. You're all right going up the hill this side of it, because you can always turn round and come back; but once you get over the brow, you slip down the other side with nothing to stop you.
INFORMATIVE. Oh no, no, I must correct you there. Technically—
GLOOMY (*turning away*). I must sit down. My doctor warned me not to stand too long or I might have another of my turns. I don't want you lot carrying me up the cliff in a blanket; you might do me more harm than good. (*Sits on high rock, near* KNITTER, *and writes postcards.*)
KNITTER. 107, 108, 109 . . .
CHEERY. Well, I'm going to have a paddle. (*Sits on small rock* L., *and takes shoes off.*)
INFORMATIVE (*reading*). In the rock pools one may discover crabs, welks, shrimps, and even an occasional jellyfish. (*Sits on low rock* R.)
MOTHER (*off*). Oo—oo! Is this the way down?
YOUNG. Yes, come on; it's lovely.
ANXIOUS. Oh dear, it's that Mrs. Whatsit, with those two awful children. (*Sits by* CHEERY *on rock* L.)
CHEERY. Well, why not? It's their outing as much as ours.
INFORMATIVE. There I would disagree. Technically the outing is a Club Outing, and children are allowed to come only as a special concession.
YOUNG. Well, they are coming, anyway.

    (*Enter* THE MOTHER, *up* L., *with two imaginary children—* "GEORGIE" *and* "JACQUELINE".)

MOTHER. Come along you two. Here we are at the seaside, and if you can't stop quarrelling I'll bang your heads together. Now go

and play on your own. Go on, Mummy doesn't want you; she just wants to sit down and have a rest.
INFORMATIVE. Come and sit here, if you like.
MOTHER. Thank you. (*Sits by* INFORMATIVE, *on low rock* R.) Georgie, take your shoes and socks off if you want to paddle. You help him Jacqueline, you're big enough. (*To the others.*) Cor, talk about helpless kids!
KNITTER. 121, 122, 123 . . .
CHEERY. I must say, I like children myself.
MOTHER. You're welcome to mine, any day.
INFORMATIVE. Of course, families in these days are not really big enough, you know. I was one of seven, and we never quarrelled.
ANXIOUS. There were four of us.
YOUNG. I think three is the best number, myself.
INFORMATIVE. Well, let's just take a vote on the ideal number for a family. You say three, I say seven. What about you?
MOTHER. I say two is too many.
ANXIOUS. I shall say four.
INFORMATIVE (*to* KNITTER). What do you say?
KNITTER. 137 . . .
INFORMATIVE. Oh, she's hopeless. (*To* MOTHER.) Where's everybody else gone?
MOTHER. They are round the corner in the next bay; the bus driver said we could go down either way. (*Calling.*) Georgie, put that seaweed down! . . . All right, sit over there and pop the little bladders if you want to, but don't wave it about.
INFORMATIVE (*looking up cliff path*). Here come some more of them. Oh, it's the President (*Or* "Chairman," "Leader," "Her Ladyship," *etc.*) and the Secretary.
CHEERY. There now, and I've just got my shoes and stockings off. Well, never mind, we are supposed to be enjoying ourselves.
  (*Enter the* PRESIDENT *and the* SECRETARY, *up* L.)
PRESIDENT. Ah, there you are. (*Coming down* C., *and looking round.*) What a delightful spot.
SECRETARY (*coming down* C., *and taking a camera from a case*). Pretty. Very pretty.
PRESIDENT (*indicating the two* OLDEST RESIDENTS). Are these—er—
INFORMATIVE. We found them here.
PRESIDENT (*whispering*). Oh, really.
INFORMATIVE. You needn't whisper; they are fast asleep.
PRESIDENT. Poor dear things. I wonder how old they are?
KNITTER. 155, 156 . . .
PRESIDENT. Surely not!—Oh, I see, you've brought some work with you.
  (KNITTER *nods without looking up.*)
SECRETARY. Now I'd just like to take a few snaps. Whereabouts is the sun? (*Manoeuvres round, squinting upwards, to get best position.*)

SEA SIDE TRIPPERS

MOTHER. Jacqueline! *(Louder.)* Jack-er-leen, mind what you're doing! . . . Well, if you wet them, you'll have to go home without any, because that's the only pair you've got. *(They all look at her.)* I only bought her those shoes last week.
SECRETARY *(aiming camera at audience).* Now first of all, one of the sea. *(Gazing out intently.)* Oh look, look, there's a porpoise.
ALL *(peering eagerly).* Where? Where?
SECRETARY. It's gone for the moment. Oh, I haven't seen a porpoise for years. There it is again; it looks just like an old man with a bald head.
PRESIDENT *(disapprovingly).* It *is* an old man with a bald head.
SECRETARY. Oh, so it is. Never mind. *(Takes photo.)* There; that's got one picture. *(Turns film on.)* Now one of the cliff.
MOTHER. Georgie! Come here. Where's your handkerchief? . . . On the bus? What's the use of leaving it up there? All right, you'd better use mine. *(Produces large hanky.)* Don't touch it with sandy fingers; here, blow. *(Leans towards audience, takes imaginary child's nose in handkerchief and wipes it.)* That's better. Run along.
KNITTER. 174, 175, 176 . . .
INFORMATIVE. How about taking a picture of *us,* while you are about it?
SECRETARY. Oh yes, indeed, I want to. *(Takes one of cliff and turns film on.)* I think that good snaps are the most important part of an outing, don't you?
GLOOMY. *Good* ones, yes.
PRESIDENT. Hullo, I didn't see you over there. What are you doing?
GLOOMY. Writing my postcards.
PRESIDENT. What a lot of them. Do you send them to all your friends?
GLOOMY. Not my friends, no, I send them to my neighbours; it makes them jealous.
MOTHER. Hullo, here comes trouble again. Well Jacqueline, what do you want now? . . . Well, you should have gone when everyone else did . . . All right then, get behind those bushes. *(To others.)* It always affects her like that when she puts her feet into cold water.
SECRETARY. Now could I have everybody together in a little group, please? *(They all start to form group in front of high rock* R.*)* That's right. *(To* PRESIDENT.*)* Would you sit in the middle? Thank you. *(They shuffle into position.)* And will you come a bit further this way . . . *(Etc., ad lib.)* Right, that should do well.
INFORMATIVE. Did you remember to turn the film on?
SECRETARY. Oh. Did I? I don't know. Yes, I think I did. I'm not sure. Number one was the sea; number two was the cliff; this should be number three. *(Examining camera.)* Let's see now, it says number—
KNITTER. 201, 202 . . .

SECRETARY. No, we're all right, it says number three. Now, are we ready?
MOTHER. Half a tick. (*Calling.*) Jacqueline, hurry up. Georgie, come here. Now sit down here in front of me, and if either of you move I'll crown you.
SECRETARY (*peering into camera sight*). Can you get any closer together? (*They try, without success.*) Well, I shall have to get further away then. (*Walks backwards, getting nearer to the edge of the stage.*)
ANXIOUS. Mind! You're walking into the sea!

(ALL *give a shriek as* SECRETARY *obviously gets feet wet.*)

SECRETARY. There now, I've got my feet wet. Oh how cold it is! Whatever shall I do?
MOTHER (*threateningly*). Jacqueline, I've told you not to use that word. It's rude.
INFORMATIVE (*to* SECRETARY). Get your shoes off quickly. Who's got a towel? (*Someone produces a towel.*) That's right; now rub your feet hard. The shoes will soon dry in the sun. Borrow these plimsols.
ANXIOUS. But what about the photograph?
INFORMATIVE. I suggest we take a group of everybody together, when we get back to the bus. And now let's have our sandwiches, shall we? It must be lunch time.

(ALL *agree, get packets from their belongings, open them and hand them round—*" . . . have one of mine . . .," " . . . these are egg . . .," " . . . I made these sausage rolls myself . . .," " . . . I never eat meat at all . . ." *Etc., ad lib.*)

I tell you what: shall we pool all our sandwiches together and then help ourselves from the pool?

(*General assent—*" . . . good idea . . .," " . . . much nicer . . .," " . . . makes it more interesting . . ." etc. MOTHER *slaps the imaginary* GEORGIE *with an* "Oh no, you don't!" *etc. They pile all the food into the lid of a large cardboard box.*)

That's the idea.
YOUNG. I say, what about the others?
INFORMATIVE. What others?
YOUNG. There should be three more of the party somewhere.
PRESIDENT. Oh yes, they are round in the next bay.
CHEERY. Well, we've got their sandwiches in this lot, so we hadn't better start until they get here.
INFORMATIVE. Let's all go and find them, shall we?
CHEERY. Good idea; and I've got a little bottle of something in the bus. We can collect that on the way. (*Slips shoes on.* ALL *prepare to go.*)
INFORMATIVE. Somebody had better stay and look after the coats and things.
CHEERY. And the sandwiches.

SEA SIDE TRIPPERS

INFORMATIVE (*to* MOTHER). Would you like to stay? I'm sure the children would rather play on the beach than come for a walk.
MOTHER. Yes, I'll stay and mind the things. Off you go, all of you, but don't be too long, will you?
INFORMATIVE. No, no, we'll just go to the top of the cliff and call them. Come along everybody.
KNITTER (*as they go*). 289, 290, 291, 292 . . .
    (*Exeunt up* L. *all except* MOTHER, *who gets comfortably settled, and then suddenly starts up, looking off* R.)
MOTHER. Georgie, come down off that rock. You can't get down? You'll get down quick enough when I reach you, my lad. No, don't you move, Mummy's coming. (*Goes out* R.)
ADVENTUROUS ONE (*off*). Hullo! Where are you?
    (*Enter down* L., *the* ADVENTUROUS ONE, *the* HUNGRY ONE *and the* READER, *all in bare feet—or beach shoes—and carrying shoes and stockings with other luggage. The* HUNGRY ONE *is eating an apple, and the* READER *is reading a book.*)
Well I'm blest, they're not here at all.
HUNGRY. No, but they've left their things here, so they must be coming back. Let's sit down a bit.
    (*They sit,* ADVENTUROUS *on rock* R., HUNGRY *on ground* C., READER *on rock* L.)
I reckon we took a big risk coming round the bottom of that cliff, didn't we?
ADVENTUROUS. Oh, I don't know; the tide's still going out. (*To* READER.) Don't you ever stop reading?
READER. Eh? Oh, I'm sorry, I was just finishing a story—it's very exciting.
ADVENTUROUS. Go on then, read us a bit.
READER (*reading*). Slowly his cool hand crept round her warm shoulders and the hot blood surged through her icy veins. His fiery breath stirred the flaming curls on her snowy neck, and the next moment his burning kisses engulfed her frozen lips.
HUNGRY. Ooh! It makes me go hot and cold all over.
ADVENTUROUS. Just a minute. (*Gets up and examines* OLDEST RESIDENTS, *and sits again.*) It's a good thing they're asleep or you might have given them blood pressure. Fancy people writing stories like that! Disgusting, I call it. (*Settling down.*) Well, go on reading.
READER. That's the end.
ADVENTUROUS. The end! Honestly, you are the limit. I was just beginning to get interested. Do you mean to tell me it ends with those burning kisses on her frozen lips?
READER (*looking at book*). Yes—except that there's a row of dots across the page after that.
ADVENTUROUS (*knowingly*). Ah, I thought there would be.
    (HUNGRY ONE *throws an imaginary stone at the audience.*)
What are you doing?

HUNGRY (*throwing another*). Throwing stones in the sea.
ADVENTUROUS. I bet I can throw one further than you.
HUNGRY. I bet you can't.
ADVENTUROUS. All right then. (*Throws.*) Beat that then.
HUNGRY (*throwing*). There!
ADVENTUROUS (*getting up and selecting a better imaginary stone*). This will beat you anyway. (*Throws.*)
HUNGRY (*getting up and throwing*). How about *that* then?
    (*They go on throwing ad lib., with suitable comments—*"Mine went beyond the second wave . . .," "I nearly hit that seagull . . .," "Look, there's a bottle; let's try and break it . . ." *etc.*)
READER (*who has left book on rock, and is looking at the heap left by the others*). I say, it looks as though they've left some sandwiches for us. (*Lifts box and shows them.*)
HUNGRY (*taking box*). Oh good, I'm hungry.
ADVENTUROUS. They've left rather a lot, haven't they?
HUNGRY. No, we can soon get through these. The sea air always gives me an appetite.
READER. Let's take them with us and walk back the way we came.
HUNGRY. That's right, and we can eat them as we go. (*Biting a sandwich.*) Come on.
ADVENTUROUS (*as they go off down* L.). I wish I knew where the others had gone. (*Goes out.*)
READER. It doesn't matter; we shall see them at tea-time. (*Goes out.*)
HUNGRY. And that won't be long now, thank goodness. (*Goes out.*)
    (*Re-enter* MOTHER, R.)
MOTHER (*to the imaginary* GEORGIE). Seagulls eggs? I'll give you seagulls eggs, you little horror. Now go and play on the sand, and stay where I can see you. (*Sees sandwiches have gone.*) Oh glory, where have the sandwiches gone? Jack-er-leen! Come here. Have you been at them sandwiches? Tell Mummy the truth now. Open your mouth and let me look. Oh gracious, here come the others back.
    (*Re-enter all the others of the first party, up* L.)
INFORMATIVE. They weren't there. There's nobody in the next bay at all. They must have gone.
MOTHER. So have our sandwiches.
ALL. What?
MOTHER. I only left them for a moment to fetch young Georgie off the rocks, and when I came back, they'd disappeared.
    (ALL *search, making ad lib. comments—*" . . . they were just here . . .," "couldn't have walked away . . .," " . . . I don't trust those kids . . .," *etc.*)
INFORMATIVE. I say, you don't think—(*indicates* OLDEST RESIDENTS.)—?
YOUNG. What a lark! (*Going close to* OLDEST RESIDENT, R.) No, I don't think so.

SEA SIDE TRIPPERS

CHEERY *(close to* SECOND OLDEST RESIDENT, L.*)*. No, it couldn't have been them.
ANXIOUS *(up* C.*)*. Could it have been smugglers? (ALL *stare.*) I mean—burglars—or—anyone?
INFORMATIVE. Well, of course it must have been someone. *(Spotting book on rock* L.*)* Hullo, what's this? A clue I think.
SECRETARY. Yes, yes, I know whose book that is.
INFORMATIVE. So do I. The others must have been here. But how could they get here without our meeting them?
MOTHER. Jacqueline, have you seen anybody come round here? . . . Three of them, eh? . . . Where did they come from? . . . Oh, round the bottom of the cliff, did they?
INFORMATIVE. Well, that solves the mystery.
READER *(off, up* L.*)*. Oo—oo! (ALL *look up.*)
INFORMATIVE *(pointing up to top of cliff, off)*. There they are. *(Calling.)* Did you take the sandwiches?
READER *(off)*. Yes, thank you.
HUNGRY *(off)*. And they were very nice too.
INFORMATIVE *(calling)*. But we haven't had any yet!
(ALL *make exclamations of surprise and alarm.*)
ADVENTUROUS *(off)*. Come on up. The driver says if we go now, we shall have time to do some shopping before tea. He'll take us straight to Woolworths and Marks and Spencers.
INFORMATIVE. Come along then, we'd better go. Gather everything up.
ANXIOUS. Oh dear, this is not a very pleasant outing, is it? *(Goes out up* L.*)*
CHEERY. Cheer up, it might have been pouring with rain all day. *(Goes out.)*
GLOOMY. I wish it had. As it is, I've brought my umbrella for nothing. *(Goes out.)*
PRESIDENT *(to* SECRETARY*)*. You'd better bring your shoes. *(Goes out.)*
SECRETARY *(picking up shoes)*. Oh, someone has filled them with sand! *(Goes out.)*
MOTHER. Jackerleen, did you touch them shoes? I'll tan the hide off you. Yes I will—and you, Georgie. Get up that path the pair of you, or I'll give you both to a policeman. *(Goes out.)*
YOUNG *(picking up last bundle)*. I think that's the lot. *(Goes out.)*
KNITTER. 397, 398, 399. Oh dear.
INFORMATIVE. What's the matter?
KNITTER. There should be 400. I must have dropped a stitch somewhere.
INFORMATIVE. Well, we can't go back and look for it now. Come along. *(They both go off.)*
SECOND OLDEST RESIDENT *(waking up after a few seconds, and leaning over.)* Eh?—er—was that you?
OLDEST RESIDENT *(stirring)*. What's that?

SEA SIDE TRIPPERS

SECOND OLDEST RESIDENT. Did you say something just now?
OLDEST RESIDENT. Did I? Oh yes, I was just going to say: What a lovely quiet spot this is.

BLACK-OUT OR QUICK CURTAIN

PRODUCTION NOTES

Sea Side Trippers, like its predecessor *Spring Song Singers*, has been specially written for quick learning and easy staging, and requires few rehearsals.

Scenery is quite unnecessary, and a few large notices will be found very effective: for example, on the back wall of the stage could be a placard printed—"THE CLIFFS," or if you prefer it—"DO NOT DAMAGE THESE CLIFFS. PENALTY £5", etc. The rocks, if they are suitably draped, should be fairly obvious; but just to make quite sure, you could erect a notice board on top, stating—"IT IS DANGEROUS TO DIVE OFF THESE ROCKS," or something similar.

Costumes can vary from the sublime to the ridiculous: The YOUNG ONE will probably favour something rather smart in beach-wear, while the GLOOMY ONE will almost certainly wear a winter coat. The rest can be as colourful or atrocious as they like.

THE OLDEST RESIDENTS must keep quite still during all the time that the other characters are on the stage, but if they are turned well away, and sufficiently concealed from the audience, there is no reason why one or both of them should not have books, and act as prompters. The INFORMATIVE ONE can also conceal a copy of the script inside the guide book, if desired. Nobody else has more than twelve lines to learn, except the MOTHER, and she has only sixteen.

In the stage directions, everybody's entrance and exit takes place on the Left, except for the few minutes that the MOTHER disappears on the Right. If your stage has more room in the wings on the other side, then merely change everything round the other way, and make your main entrance up R. It would be also quite effective to let the ADVENTUROUS, HUNGRY and READER enter from *outside* the proscenium arch and climb up on to the stage, as if they had been wading through the water.

Sea Side Trippers can be performed with a mixed cast, or with a cast of all the same sex. What fun it would be to put it on with an entirely male cast!

R.T.

www.ingramcontent.com/pod-product-compliance
Lightning Source LLC
Chambersburg PA
CBHW061953070426
42450CB00012BA/3304